HOW SCRIPTURE CAME TO US

Study by Michael L. Ruffin
Commentary by Guy Sayles

Free downloadable Teaching Guide for this study available at

NextSunday.com/teachingguides

NextSunday Resources
6316 Peake Road
Macon, Georgia 31210-3960
1-800-747-3016
©2021 by NextSunday Resources

TABLE OF CONTENTS

How Scripture Came to Us

HOW TO USE THIS STUDY

NextSunday Resources Adult Bible Studies are designed to help adults study Scripture seriously within the context of the larger Christian tradition and, through that process, find their faith renewed, challenged, and strengthened. We study the Scriptures because we believe they affect our current lives in important ways. Each study contains the following three components:

Study Guide

Each study guide lesson is arranged in four movements:

Reflecting recalls a contemporary story, anecdote, example, or illustration to help us anticipate the session's relevance in our lives.

Studying is centered on giving the biblical material in-depth attention while often surrounding it with helpful insights from theology, ethics, church history, and other areas.

Understanding helps us find relevant connections between our lives and the biblical message.

What About Me? provides brief statements that help unite life issues with the meaning of the biblical text.

Commentary

Each study guide lesson is accompanied by an additional, in-depth commentary on the biblical material. Written by a different author than the study guide, each commentary gives the opportunity for learners to approach the Scripture text from a separate but complementary viewpoint.

Teaching Guide

In addition to the provided study guide and commentary, *NextSunday Resources* also provides a *free* downloadable teaching guide, available at NextSunday.com. Each teaching guide gives the teacher tools for focusing on the content of each study guide lesson through additional commentary and Bible background information. Through teacher helps and teaching options, each teaching guide also provides substance for variety and choice in the preparation of each lesson.

NextSunday
Resources

STUDY INTRODUCTION

This unit is partly about how Scripture *came* to us. Along the way, we will look at how the Bible developed from its roots in oral tradition to collections of written texts and finally to the biblical canon we now have. We will also look at how the Bible came to be translated from Hebrew and Greek into other ancient languages, such as English. We will seek to develop greater appreciation for all the work that was done by the preachers and teachers who spoke the word, the collectors and editors who expanded and organized the word, the scribes who copied, preserved, and protected the word, and the translators who translated the word. We will also seek to develop a greater appreciation for the God who inspired the word.

We will also hopefully grow in our appreciation for the God who stands behind and within the word, for the Christ who fulfills it, and for the Spirit who enlivens it. All of that is going on right here and now, so this unit is also about how Scripture *comes* to us. Its words come to us as we make ourselves available to them by carefully and prayerfully studying them. In those words, we find ourselves drawn more and more into the life of God and into life with God.

We are grateful for the great gift of our Bible, but what do we do with that great gift? Do we show our appreciation for it in the amount of attention that we give it? Do we approach it with an attitude of humility, asking God to help us understand what we need to understand, or do we come to it with an attitude of arrogance that assumes we already know what we need to know? Do we read our Bibles through the lens of Jesus, desiring that our study of the Bible will lead us to a life characterized by the kind of love he showed us and that only he can make possible in us?

Yes, Scripture not only came to us; it also comes to us.

Thanks be to God who made and makes it all possible—and to all the people who worked and work with God to make it all possible!

1

SCRIBES
AND SCRIPTURES
Jeremiah 36:4-8, 20-26, 32; Luke 1:1-4

Central Question
How is the Bible both human and divine?

Scripture

Jeremiah 36:4-8, 20-26, 32
4 So Jeremiah sent for Baruch, Neriah's son. As Jeremiah dictated all the words that the Lord had spoken to him, Baruch wrote them in the scroll. 5 Then Jeremiah told Baruch, "I'm confined here and can't go to the Lord's temple. 6 So you go to the temple on the next day of fasting, and read the Lord's words from the scroll that I have dictated to you. Read them so that all the people in the temple can hear them, as well as all the Judeans who have come from their towns. 7 If they turn from their evil ways, perhaps the Lord will hear their prayers. The Lord has threatened them with fierce anger." 8 Baruch, Neriah's son, did everything the prophet Jeremiah instructed him: he read all the Lord's words from the scroll in the temple.... 20 After leaving the scroll in the room of Elishama the scribe, they went to the king's court and told him everything. 21 The king sent Jehudi to take the scroll, and he retrieved it from the room of Elishama the scribe. Then Jehudi read it to the king and all his royal officials who were standing next to the king. 22 Now it was the ninth month, and the king was staying in the winterized part of the palace with the firepot burning near him. 23 And whenever Jehudi read three or four columns of the scroll, the king would cut them off with a scribe's knife and throw them into the firepot until the whole scroll was burned up. 24 Neither the king nor any of his attendants

who heard all these words were alarmed or tore their clothes. 25 Elnathan, Delaiah, and Gemariah begged the king not to burn the scroll, but he wouldn't listen to them. 26 The king commanded Jerahmeel, the king's son, along with Seraiah, Azriel's son, and Shelemiah, Abdeel's son, to arrest the scribe Baruch and the prophet Jeremiah. But the Lord hid them.... 32 So Jeremiah took another scroll and gave it to the scribe Baruch, Neriah's son, who wrote at Jeremiah's dictation all the words in the scroll burned in the fire by Judah's King Jehoiakim. Many similar words were added to them.

Luke 1:1-4
1 Many people have already applied themselves to the task of compiling an account of the events that have been fulfilled among us. 2 They used what the original eyewitnesses and servants of the word handed down to us. 3 Now, after having investigated everything carefully from the beginning, I have also decided to write a carefully ordered account for you, most honorable Theophilus. 4 I want you to have confidence in the soundness of the instruction you have received.

Reflecting

When you read a novel, do you give any thought to the process by which it came into existence? Do you wonder how the writer created it? Do you want to find out what sources she used and how she used them? Do you want to look for evidence of an editor's hand? The answer to all of those questions is probably "No" because you are interested in the finished product and not in the history of the book's development.

? Do you know anyone who writes (other than the occasional thank-you note)? Have you ever considered what goes into writing a book or article for publication?

It is understandable if we tend to think of our Bible in the same way. After all, the Bible that we read has been a completed work for a very long time; the Old Testament canon was established by the first century AD and the New Testament canon by the fourth century. Although we know work is still being done on translations, we nonetheless tend to think of the Bible as a finished product.

Why, then, should we care about how the Bible came to be? Let's consider two reasons. First, the Bible cares about how the Bible came to be. That is, there are stories told, such as in this week's Jeremiah text, and there are statements made, such as in this week's Luke text, that lead us to think about the development of the Bible.

Second, the story of how the Bible came to be is also the story of how God partnered with humanity in working out God's process of reconciling the world to God's self, a story that reaches its climax with the ultimate divine-human partnership, the coming of Jesus Christ to the world. The story of the Bible and the story of God's working in and through humanity are one story—the story of salvation.

Studying

The book of Jeremiah begins, "These are the words of Jeremiah.... The Lord's word came to Jeremiah in the thirteenth year of Judah's King Josiah" (1:1-2). So we are told up front that Jeremiah's book contains both "the words of Jeremiah" and "the Lord's word." While it is reasonable to conclude that Jeremiah's words resulted from his reception of God's word, it is also reasonable to conclude that the words in the book resulted from the interaction between the Lord, the prophet, the people to whom the words were addressed, and the historical situations in which these words were spoken, written, edited, and preserved. This week's Jeremiah text offers us evidence that supports that conclusion.

At the beginning of Jeremiah 36, we learn that "in the fourth year of Judah's King Jehoiakim, Josiah's son, this word came to Jeremiah from the Lord" (v. 1). That year was 605 BC, the year that Nebuchadnezzar and the Babylonians defeated Necho and the Egyptians at Carchemish, a victory that established Babylonian supremacy in the region and made it clear that Babylon would be an ongoing threat to Judah. So the word of the Lord came to the prophet during, and probably in response to, a specific set of historical circumstances.

The word of the Lord also came to the prophet as an effort to bridge the divide between God and God's people. The people of Judah were in serious trouble because of their sin. They desperately needed to repent if they were going to have any chance of avoiding the impending Babylonian disaster. God's word said that Jeremiah was to produce a written scroll of the preaching that he had done from the beginning of his ministry around 627 BC (see 1:2) until that time. As stated by God (v. 2) and repeated in Jeremiah's instructions to Baruch to read it publicly (v. 7), the reason for producing the scroll was to create an opportunity for the people to repent. This would in turn open up the possibility of God cancelling the coming judgment. The scroll contained good news even in its words of judgment, then, because it offered the people the opportunity to heal the wound in their relationship with God.

> The purpose of the scroll...is to move Judah to hear... and to turn..., and so to avoid evil. That is, the scroll is not designed to give information, nor even to make an argument, but it is to authorize, energize, and evoke a transformed life. (Brueggemann, 346)

So writing down the prophet's preaching was a part of God's effort to lead the people to repentance and to covenant faithfulness. In other words, it was an aspect of God's saving activity in the world. Although Jeremiah didn't know he was producing Scripture, the purpose of his written scroll had the same purpose that Scripture has, according to 2 Timothy 3:16-17: equipping God's people for lives of faithfulness.

The opening words of Luke indicate that the purpose of Luke's Gospel was also related to the saving activity of God. Luke says that he wrote his account so that Theophilus (and no doubt other readers) would be able to "have confidence in the soundness of the instruction" that he gained from the book (Luke 1:4). To that end, Luke says that he expended much effort and made use of every available resource in order to

> Every scripture is inspired by God and is useful for teaching, for showing mistakes, for correcting, and for training character, so that the person who belongs to God can be equipped to do everything that is good. (2 Tim 3:16-17)

produce the most dependable account of the life of Jesus possible. That meant that he used the previously produced written sources to which he had access, including the Gospel of Mark (half of which appears in Luke) and other documents. God worked through Luke's use of sources and his meticulous efforts at producing a "carefully ordered account" (1:3) to communicate the good news of Jesus Christ.

One reason for writing down the word of the Lord was to preserve it. This didn't necessarily ensure its protection, however. When Jeremiah's scribe Baruch, the one who actually wrote down the words dictated by the prophet, read the scroll to the people, some court officials made sure that the scroll made its way to King Jehoiakim. But when the scroll was read to the king, he cut it up piece by piece and burned it in the fire that burned before him as he sat in one of the winterized rooms of his palace. His act of destruction constituted a blatant rejection of the word of God that came to him in Jeremiah's scroll.

But, as Brueggemann notes, "The scroll is so much more difficult to resist because it cannot, like a person, be intimidated, banished, or destroyed. It keeps reappearing" (346). And so the word of the Lord came again to the prophet in response to the rejection of that word. God told Jeremiah to produce another scroll (36:27-28). Once again, Jeremiah dictated the message scroll to Baruch, but this scroll contained "many similar words" in addition to those that were on the first scroll (v. 32).

Here we have a story that tells of the beginning stages of the book of Jeremiah. It developed from the oral tradition of the preaching of the prophet to a first edition of a scroll to the second edition of a scroll. There were many other additions and editions as well. The book of Jeremiah as a whole displays evidence of a very long and complicated textual history.

For example, the fact that it closes with material that is also found in 2 Kings 24:18–25:30 is the most obvious proof it was worked on by editors during or after the Babylonian Exile (c. 587–538 BC).

Also, manuscripts found among the Dead Sea Scrolls reveal that during the two centuries leading up to the time of Christ, the Hebrew text of Jeremiah still existed in at least two forms, one of which is reflected in the Masoretic text, the Hebrew text that is the basis of our English Old Testament, and one of which is reflected in the Septuagint, the Greek translation of the Old Testament that was the Bible of the early church.

Understanding

This week's Scripture texts teach us some important things about how the Bible came to be.

First, the Bible came to be through the initiative of God. Before Jeremiah dictated the contents of the scroll for Baruch to write, "this word came to Jeremiah from the Lord" (Jer 36:1). Although we are not told how that act of inspiration worked, we are told that God is the ultimate originator of what we find in our Bibles.

Second, the Bible came to be through the efforts of human beings. Jeremiah spoke, and Baruch wrote. Luke collected and sifted his sources. God worked in partnership with all of them, and they worked in partnership with each other to produce the Bible.

Third, the Bible came to be under specific historical circumstances. Our Bible bears witness to God's activity in history. God graciously comes into the circumstances of our lives to bring the word, which is an aspect of God's saving activity in the world. In both of this week's texts, we see how historical circumstances contributed to the production of writings that became part of Scripture.

Fourth, the Bible came to be through a process of revision and expansion. After Jehoiakim destroyed Jeremiah and Baruch's first scroll, they produced an expanded one. Luke said that his work was an expansion and revision of previous efforts at telling the story of Jesus. Many of the books of the Bible show evidence of editorial activity, some over extended periods of time.

Fifth, the Bible came to be through a process of discernment. Luke believed that he could improve on what had been written before. Over the centuries during which the Bible came into being, many decisions were made by many people concerning how best to organize and present the material that now constitutes the Bible.

Sixth, the Bible came to be through a process of survival. Jehoiakim rejected the word of the Lord. Countless others have rejected it, too, and have even tried, like Jehoiakim, to destroy it. Yet it has survived.

What About Me?

• *What assumptions have I had about how the Bible came to be?* Do I need to revise how I think about the Bible? What difference does my understanding of the Bible's origin and development make for my faith and for my witness?

• *How should I think about what happens when I study the Bible?* Since the Bible came about through a divine-human partnership, what does this mean for how I approach Scripture? When I come to it, is there still a divine-human interaction taking place? Do I pray before I read the Bible? Do I pray while I am studying the Bible? Am I open to the Spirit's leadership as I study it?

• *How is Bible-reading a community experience?* The production of the Bible was a community undertaking: Jeremiah and Baruch worked together. Luke used previous writers' material and wrote to address the needs of the church. The church determined what books would and wouldn't be in the canon. How, then, do my sisters and brothers in Christ help inform my reading and understanding of the Bible?

• *Do I appreciate what it took to put a Bible in my hands?* God not only inspired the writers of Scripture but made sure it would survive until today. This took not only bold prophets such as Jeremiah but also faithful scribes such as Baruch, thoughtful author-editors such as Luke, and capable translators down through the centuries. How does my handling of (and obedience to) Scripture reflect gratitude for this amazing God-directed process?

Resource

Walter Brueggemann, *A Commentary on Jeremiah: Exile & Homecoming* (Grand Rapids MI: Eerdmans, 1998).

SCRIBES
AND SCRIPTURES
Jeremiah 36:4-8, 20-26, 32; Luke 1:1-4

Cherished Bibles

In this lesson, as well as the next three, we remind ourselves of the wonder and significance of the Bible: of the gift it is to us and of the relationship with God it serves. Today, we marvel at some of the ways in which the Scriptures are both human and divine—both "a" book and "the" Book.

On a bookshelf in my study, there are three Bibles that have special significance for me. First, there's a small New Testament bound in stiff imitation leather with a fold-over flap with a clasp. My grandparents gave it to me on my birthday, which was just a few days after my baptism. On the inside, written in now-fading blue ink, there's this inscription: "For Guy, on his eighth birthday, as he grows in his faith. From your grandparents, Hearvy and Gladys Sayles."

Next, there's a King James Version Bible with silver-edged pages and supple calfskin leather. Crestview Baptist Church in Griffin, Georgia, gave it to me when I was ordained. It's a tangible reminder that a calling to ministry both rises from and answers to the community of faith.

Finally, there's a tattered paperback copy of *The Cotton Patch Version of Paul's Letters*, translated by farmer and New Testament scholar Clarence Jordan into the mindset, vocabulary, and geography of the mid-twentieth century American South. The glue that once held the pages in place has dried out, the binding is broken, and many of the pages are coffee-stained. A college English professor who had also become a friend gave me Jordan's version of Paul's writings. They helped me see myself, my culture, and my faith in ways that both convicted and inspired me.

I cherish these Bibles both because of the sacred literature they are and because of their ties to people who nurtured my faith. As important as those copies of Scripture are to me, it would be a mistake for me to think that their greatest value is as objects—as commemorative keepsakes to remind me of people and experiences that have been important to me. The Bible has limited value as a possession or an icon. Its greater value is when we let it guide and catalyze a living relationship with God.

Many other Bibles in various versions sit on that shelf in my study. Among the translations I have are: Today's English Version (which, in my childhood, was called "Good News for Modern Man"), the New International Version, the Revised— and New Revised—Standard Versions, the New English Bible, the Jerusalem Bible, the Common English Bible, and Eugene Peterson's *The Message*. I have easy access to these and an array of other translations of the Scriptures—so easy that I sometimes forget what a complicated and amazing gift it is to have a reliably translated and pleasantly readable Bible.

Translating the Scriptures

A translation of the Scriptures involves establishing the Hebrew, Aramaic, and Greek texts from which the translation will be made. There are no original manuscripts of any of the books of the Bible, and there are rarely complete manuscripts of a particular book. Instead, there are partial, sometimes even fragmentary, manuscripts. Scholars who practice textual criticism compare these manuscripts ("texts") to each other, choose the wording that seems likeliest to reflect the original, and assemble a final text from which to do the work of translation. As new sources are discovered, scholars may suggest modifications of the texts from which our translations are made. The constant goal is to have a baseline text that is as close to the elusive original as possible.

Since every translation inevitably involves interpretation, it's crucial to have more than one translator working on a text. That's why translators rarely work as individuals. Rather, they work in teams in order to reduce the possibility that a translation will bear the marks of individual bias and to increase the likelihood that it will be as objective as possible.

Early in their work, translators face an important decision: whether to attempt a word-by-word or a thought-by-thought translation. A word-by-word (or "formal equivalency") translation is more literal, but there are some words in the original languages that have no direct counterpart in English. A thought-by-thought (or "dynamic equivalency") translation can be more easily understood by a reader, but in this kind of translation the line between translating a text and interpreting it can be blurred even further than it already is in a word-by-word translation. Many translations are a kind of hybrid: they are as word-by-word as possible, but resort to thought-by-thought when a more literal translation is either simply impossible or would be unnecessarily confusing.

Translators also have to decide what level of the receptor language (in our case, English) to use. Is this a translation for a beginning reader? Sixth grade? High school graduate? They also need to be clear about the cultural and church contexts of their most probable readers. Do those readers live, for instance, in rural areas, where passages like the agricultural parables of Jesus will find readier resonance? Or, do those readers live in primarily urban environments, where the imagery of grazing sheep, fatted calves, and fields ready for harvest will sound alien?

With this brief description, I've significantly oversimplified the translation process. Even with this broad-brush sketch, however, we can see what a complex and painstaking process the production of an English translation of the Bible can be. It involves painstaking scholarship, familiarity with the original languages of the Bible, cultural sensitivity, skillful writing, and spiritual discernment. Our ability to read the written word of God, as the Bible is sometimes called, depends on the devout and disciplined labor of men and women. The divine word reaches us through human instruments.

The Scriptures Are a Divine-Human Partnership

In the Scriptures themselves, we see signs of the divine-human partnership (sometimes the divine-human tension) by which the Bible came to exist. In Jeremiah 36, for example, we read of God commanding Jeremiah to write the words God had spoken to him about "Israel, Judah, and all the nations from the time of Josiah until today" (Jer 36:2). King Josiah reigned in Israel from 639–609 BC, and Jeremiah began his prophetic ministry in the thirteenth year of Josiah's kingship, around 627 or 626. The command for Jeremiah to write down the words God had spoken to him came in "the fourth year of Judah's King Jehoiakim, Josiah's son" (36:1), or around 605 BC. It seems likely that those messages from God are what we know as chapters 1–25 of the book of Jeremiah.

The passage says that Jeremiah sent for Baruch, who served as a scribe or secretary to the prophet, and, "as Jeremiah dictated all the words that the Lord had spoken to him, Baruch wrote them in the scroll" (v. 4). Jeremiah then told Baruch to go to the temple on a fast-day and to read the words he had dictated to the worshippers who gathered there: "Read them so that all the people in the temple can hear them, as well as all the Judeans who have come from their towns" (v. 6). Jeremiah hoped that hearing God's words would cause the residents of Jerusalem and Judah to repent of their sins, which God was about to judge (v. 7). Baruch did as Jeremiah instructed: "He read all the Lord's words from the scroll in the temple" (v. 8).

The words of God that Baruch read from the scroll disturbed some and angered many of the royal officials in Jerusalem. When the king heard Jeremiah's words—God's words—he cut Baruch's scroll into pieces and burned them (see vv. 9-25).

With the original scroll destroyed, God ordered Jeremiah to produce another one with the same words and deliver this second scroll and its message to King Jehoiakim with the dread assurance that judgment was coming upon him (vv. 27-31). So, again, Jeremiah dictated the words to Baruch. Our text says that the second scroll contained all the words Jeremiah had spoken the first time, as well as some new ones: "Many similar words were added to them" (v. 32).

As with the book of Jeremiah, so too with other books of the Bible. They contain stories told not just once, but over and over again, and bear messages delivered on many occasions. Depending on the audience that heard the stories and messages, and also on both the memory and the creative inspiration of the speakers, those accounts could vary from each other. Details could be added or left out, elaborations could be made or summaries offered. New words could be added or familiar words that didn't need to be repeated for those who already knew them could be subtracted. The result was that several versions, or editions, of biblical books came to exist, a result that is similar to the multiple manuscripts or parts of manuscripts of Bible books with which contemporary Bible scholars work. It's such a human process—storytelling tailored to specific listeners and messages fashioned to reach particular hearers—by which God's word came to be spoken and written.

The writer of Luke's Gospel tells us that he consulted a variety of sources as he crafted his narrative about Jesus. These sources included the testimony of people who had seen and heard Jesus in his lifetime: "Many people have already applied themselves to the task of compiling an account of the events that have been fulfilled among us. They used what the original eyewitnesses and servants of the word handed down to us" (Luke 1:1-2). It's intriguing, isn't it, that there were, in the first century, before the four Gospels of our New Testament were written, already "many accounts" of the good news. Luke began the work on his own Gospel by familiarizing himself with those accounts.

Then, Luke did research of his own. He "investigated everything carefully from the beginning" (1:3). I wonder if he interviewed surviving followers of the earthly Jesus or talked to his elderly mother, Mary, or asked people who had lived in Galilee what they remembered about the words and deeds of Jesus. Luke combined what he learned from the already existing accounts of Jesus' life, teaching, death, and resurrection with the results of his own investigations and wrote "a carefully ordered account" (1:3). Luke produced a *carefully* ordered account. In other words, he exercised an artist's or an author's devotion to craft and style. Luke wrote an ordered account, which means he arranged the details of the story of Jesus in a way that helped to highlight the truths about Jesus that Luke felt were most significant. Notice again the very human process—reading, researching, arranging, and ordering material—by which the divine word comes to us.

Divine-Human *Written* Word, Divine-Human *Living* Word

The humanity and divinity of the written word of God that comes to us through the Bible reflects the humanity and divinity of the living Word of God that we encounter in Jesus, to which the Bible bears witness. Just as God was revealed in the human life of Jesus, so also is God revealed in the human speech and writing of the authors of Scripture. Just as it would be heresy to deny the humanity of Jesus, it is also wrong to deny the humanity of the Bible. The Bible is God's word revealed through human words.

Inspired as the writers were, they did their work in ways that human authors do, using and creating literary forms. They were not passive stenographers or robots who channeled the word of God in a kind of trance. They were researchers, poets, artists, and witnesses who thought about how to say what needed to be said.

God worked with those human authors, inspired their imaginations, sparked their creativity, energized their investigations, respected their capacities and limitations, and used their perspectives and experiences to shape their writing of stories, messages, instructions, and letters. Those writings, while bearing all the marks of human authorship, also speak to us with divine authority and transforming power.

Notes

Notes

2

SCHOLARS
AND TRANSLATORS
Nehemiah 8:1, 5-8; Acts 8:26-31

Central Question
Who has helped me be a better informed Bible reader?

Scripture
Nehemiah 8:1, 5-8
1 When the seventh month came and the people of Israel were settled in their towns, all the people gathered together in the area in front of the Water Gate. They asked Ezra the scribe to bring out the Instruction scroll from Moses, according to which the Lord had instructed Israel.... 5 Standing above all of the people, Ezra the scribe opened the scroll in the sight of all of the people. And as he opened it, all of the people stood up. 6 Then Ezra blessed the Lord, the great God, and all of the people answered, "Amen! Amen!" while raising their hands. Then they bowed down and worshipped the Lord with their faces to the ground. 7 The Levites—Jeshua, Bani, Sherebiah, Jamin, Akkub, Shabbethai, Hodiah, Maaseiah, Kelita, Azariah, Jozabad, Hanan, and Pelaiah—helped the people to understand the Instruction while the people remained in their places. 8 They read aloud from the scroll, the Instruction from God, explaining and inter- preting it so the people could understand what they heard.

Acts 8:26-31
26 An angel from the Lord spoke to Philip, "At noon, take the road that leads from Jerusalem to Gaza." (This is a desert road.) 27 So he did. Meanwhile, an Ethiopian man was on his way home from Jerusalem, where he had come to worship. He was

a eunuch and an official responsible for the entire treasury of Candace. (Candace is the title given to the Ethiopian queen.) 28 He was reading the prophet Isaiah while sitting in his carriage. 29 The Spirit told Philip, "Approach this carriage and stay with it." 30 Running up to the carriage, Philip heard the man reading the prophet Isaiah. He asked, "Do you really understand what you are reading?" 31 The man replied, "Without someone to guide me, how could I?" Then he invited Philip to climb up and sit with him.

Reflecting

I had the privilege of participating in a ministry experience in Kenya a few years ago. This included preaching one Sunday morning in a village church. It was my only experience to date of working with a translator. I preached in English, and the translator converted my words into Swahili. I would speak a sentence and pause while he translated. It was a fascinating experience. I found myself hoping that the translator improved upon my sermon!

When I reflected on that experience, I marveled at what was going on there. When I read the morning Scripture passage, I read from an English text that had been translated from a Greek text. Then, as I expounded on that text in English, the translator translated (and, I suspect, interpreted) my words into Swahili. I am sure that the Holy Spirit was working in both of us—indeed, in all of us who were present—to open up the Scriptures to us. And, if all went really well, the Spirit opened our minds and hearts to experience the risen Christ and to grasp the meaning of the text through the lens of Christ.

In Kenya on that day, God and people worked together to translate and interpret the Scriptures. In every place and among every people where the good news is being proclaimed, those partnerships continue.

> Whom can I ask for help in understanding the Scriptures? Who has proved a helpful guide in the past?

Studying

Philip was one of seven Greek-speaking Jewish believers set aside to ensure that Greek-speaking (as opposed to Aramaic-speaking) widows were adequately cared for in the Jerusalem church (Acts 6:1-7). When the Jerusalem church experienced persecution following the martyrdom of Stephen (8:1-3), Philip went into Samaria to preach. Being a speaker of Greek and a witness to the spread of the good news to non-Jews, he was well suited for the assignment that the Lord laid before him in today's lesson.

That assignment involved meeting an Ethiopian government official who was riding in a chariot on the desert road from Jerusalem to Gaza. Luke says he was on his way home after worshiping in Jerusalem. He was likely a "God-fearer," someone who was attracted to Judaism and worshiped the Lord but had not formally converted. He was essentially Ethiopia's Secretary of the Treasury. In Ethiopian tradition, the king was considered too exalted to carry out such mundane tasks as governing the country. Therefore, this official served the Candace, the queen mother who carried out such administrative functions (Bruce, 175).

Most likely, the scroll was the Greek version of the Old Testament, known as the Septuagint. This word means "Seventy," so called because of a tradition that seventy (or seventy-two) Jewish scholars had translated it. When Philip asked the Ethiopian if he understood what he was reading, he confessed that he didn't and that he needed someone to help him. The Ethiopian is a good model for us in his willingness to accept the help of a more experienced guide.

Philip offered a Christ-centered interpretation of the passage the Ethiopian was reading, Isaiah 53:7-8 (quoted in Acts 8:32-33). That is, he followed the early Christians' practice of looking to their Bible, the Septuagint, for passages that would help them to understand the messianic character of Jesus' life, death, and resurrection.

We do well to look for interpreters of the Bible today who understand that we encounter God in Christ through the Holy Spirit in the words of Scripture. We also do well to look for interpreters who understand that if Jesus is the center of the Bible, then he is also the lens through which the Bible is to be read and understood. If we are to take the Bible seriously as Christian Scripture, then we will take Jesus seriously as the key to meeting God in the Bible.

At the same time, we need to rely on other interpreters of the Bible to understand its nature, history, and background. We are fortunate to live in a time when biblical scholarship allows us to understand so much about the literary, historical, and social background of Scripture. We do well to avail ourselves of the expertise of those who both know God well and know God's book well.

The Ethiopian didn't need the scroll translated, but he did need it explained. By contrast, the Jews in the story told in Nehemiah 8 needed the scroll that was read to them both translated and explained. The setting of the story is the Persian province of Judah in the middle of the fifth century BC, less than a hundred years after the Jews were first allowed to return to Judah from their Babylonian exile. The priest Ezra, who had recently returned from Babylon, was asked to read a Torah scroll, most likely one that he had brought back with him, to the people. As he read it, Levites translated the words for the people. This work of interpretation was necessary because the scroll was written in Hebrew, a language the common people no longer spoke. Instead, they had adopted Aramaic, the language of the Babylonians.

The need for understanding created the necessity of translation. Such work started with these on-the-spot translations of the Old Testament from Hebrew to Aramaic. By the time of Jesus, Jewish scholars had composed written Aramaic *Targums* or paraphrases. Other important early translations of the Old Testament are the Greek Septuagint we have already mentioned and the Latin Vulgate, translated by the Christian scholar Jerome between AD 382–405.

What about English translations? Although various portions of the Bible were translated into Old English before about 1000, the first translation of the entire Bible into English was a translation from the Vulgate by students and followers of Oxford scholar John Wycliffe. Wycliffe's first edition, which was woodenly literal, was published in 1382. A second, freer edition was published in 1388.

The most influential English translation was that of William Tyndale, who produced the first printed edition of the English Bible. Tyndale published the complete New Testament in 1526, the Pentateuch in 1530, and Jonah in 1531. He was executed in 1536 before he could publish any more of the Old Testament. The tremendous influence of Tyndale's work is seen in the fact that it served as the basis for all subsequent revisions of the English Bible, including the King James Version, down through the British Revised Version of 1881–1885.

> Many works have been written on the history of the English Bible. The book by Metzger noted in the Resources is the source for the information presented in this lesson.

In fact, the King James Version of 1611 was a revision of the Bishops' Bible, which was a revision of the Great Bible, which was a revision of the Coverdale and Tyndale Bibles (Metzger, 76). As new manuscript discoveries and other advances occurred, it became necessary to revise the King James Version, a task accomplished with the British Revised Version of 1881 (New Testament) and 1885 (Old Testament) and the companion project, the American Standard Version of 1901. The American Standard Version was further revised in the Revised Standard Version (1952) and the New Revised Standard Version (1990). Again, all of these works are ultimately revisions of William Tyndale's work.

Understanding

It would be nice if we all could read the Old Testament in Hebrew and the New Testament in Greek. Even if we could, though, there would still be translation work to be done. We'd still have a lot of work to do to understand the meaning of some of the words and expressions we would encounter. And there would still be interpretive work to do. Reading requires interpretation, so even if we understood the words, we would still often need help grasping their meaning.

Fortunately, God has chosen to work with humans to ensure that we have Bibles in our own language on which we can depend. In the story of the Levites translating the Hebrew of the Torah scroll into Aramaic so the people could understand, we see an early stage of the biblical translation process. The practice of translating the Hebrew text led to the development of the Aramaic *Targums*, the Greek Septuagint, and the Latin Vulgate.

Today, we are blessed to have a Bible we can understand. Some of us may have whole shelves of Bibles in a variety of English translations. Let us thank God for the diligent work of scholars and translators who have made it possible for us to hear, read, and respond to the word of God.

What About Me?

• *How badly do we want to read the Bible?* The people asked Ezra to read them the Torah. When he began to read, they all stood up. They were eager to hear the words of the scroll and they had great respect for it. What do our actions reveal about our level of eagerness and respect for the Bible?

• *How grateful are we for the privilege of reading the Bible in our own language?* Many people labored, some of them at risk of their lives, to ensure that we would have a Bible on which we can depend. Have we thanked God for those people lately? Do we show our gratitude by faithfully reading the Bibles that they made possible?

• *How ready are we to receive the help of others in understanding the Bible?* The Jews received the help of the Levites and the Ethiopian received Philip's help. Sometimes we need help understanding the Scriptures. Do we have teachers, friends, and writers on whom we can depend for help? Do we seek them out? How do we evaluate their trustworthiness?

• *How ready are we to help others to understand the Bible?* If we have been following Jesus and studying our Bibles for some time, we should be numbered among those whom others can call on for help in understanding the Scriptures. Are we trustworthy guides? Do our lives show that we are in constant communion with the resurrected Christ so that we make him the center of our biblical interpretation?

Resources

F. F. Bruce, *The Book of Acts*, rev. ed., The New International Commentary on the New Testament (Grand Rapids MI: Eerdmans, 1988).

Richard J. Foster with Kathryn A. Helmers, *Life with God: Reading the Bible for Spiritual Formation* (New York: HarperOne, 2008).

Matthew Levering, *Ezra & Nehemiah*, Brazos Theological Commentary on the Bible (Grand Rapids MI: Brazos, 2007).

Bruce M. Metzger, *The Bible in Translation: Ancient and English Versions* (Grand Rapids MI: Baker Academic, 2001).

SCHOLARS
AND TRANSLATORS
Nehemiah 8:1, 5-8; Acts 8:26-31

Introduction

More than thirty years ago, in the dimly lit basement fellowship hall of a church in New Albany, Indiana, I heard a then-young Old Testament scholar, Walter Brueggemann, explore the opening chapters of the book of Genesis. As he spoke with passion and wisdom about how God is always making and remaking the world—and us—from chaos, those ancient words came alive for me in new and astonishing ways. This skilled and spirited teacher deepened and broadened, in lasting ways, my approach to reading and interpreting the Old Testament.

The feeling that the Scriptures were living words was similar to the feeling I had when, as an eleven-year-old boy, I heard my pastor, Ken Haag, teach a Wednesday night series of Bible studies on Paul's letter to the Philippians. There was something magical about those nights. In my imagination, I saw and heard Paul as he wrote to his friends in Philippi. I sensed his joy in them and his hopes for them. I marveled at how the humility and glory of Jesus shaped nearly everything Paul thought and did. I was on the threshold of my teenage years, during which I questioned everything I had once believed. But as a young adult, when I picked up the Bible again, I saw the notes I had written in the margins of my Bible during that study of Philippians. I remembered those Wednesday night studies, and the memories helped to rekindle my enthusiasm for reading and understanding Scripture.

What a Text Says, What It Meant, and What it Means

Walter Brueggemann, Ken Haag, seminary professors, Sunday school teachers, colleagues, and friends have all made me a better student of the Bible. So have scholars and translators whom I've never met, because they've helped me with vital tasks of interpretation that I couldn't achieve on my own. To understand the significance of a passage of Scripture, we need to know what it *says*, what it *meant* to the people who first heard or read it, and what it *could mean* to us.

Translators help us to know what a text *says*. As we saw last week, they establish the best available version of the Hebrew, Greek, or Aramaic text. And, with sensitivity to both ancient and contemporary cultures and modes of expression, they make it possible for us to read that text in our own language.

Whether they've been formally trained in a university or seminary context or they've gained their knowledge from years of personal and church-based study, biblical scholars guide us to a sense of what a passage probably *meant* to its first hearers and readers. These scholars make us aware of the likely issues and concerns that prompted the writing of a particular text, the influence a text's author hoped to have, and how that text relates to others in Scripture.

Once we know what a passage *says* and what it *meant,* we are in a position to discover what it *means*, or could mean, to us. That kind of discovery often occurs when we study the Bible with other people. Their questions and perspectives enrich our understanding, and our wonderments and opinions contribute to theirs.

It is certainly true that we can make such discoveries when we are engaged in individual reflection, and we have the right and responsibility to come to our own conclusions about the significance of a passage. Even so, the conclusions we reach about the Bible are shaped by others, perhaps in ways we don't always recognize. We are simultaneously free to interpret the Bible for ourselves, responsible to do so, and in need of the help others offer us as we exercise that freedom and responsibility.

The Levites Help the People to Understand (Neh 8:1, 5-8)

Five centuries before the life of Jesus, there was a gathering for worship on the streets of Jerusalem, near the edge of the city at a place called the Water Gate. Over a hundred years before this gathering took place, the Babylonian empire, enemies of Israel, had destroyed the city, reduced the majestic temple Solomon built to a pile of rubble, toppled the walls which surrounded the city, and taken its leading citizens into exile.

For two generations, those exiles had wondered if they'd ever go back home. Eventually, shifts of power in the region gave them the opportunity to return to the land of their memories and longings. The city to which they returned was not glorious, as it had once been. Jerusalem was grimy and desolate. Its ruins stood as a reminder of crumbled fortunes. The temple was a pile of stones and despair.

Two leaders, Nehemiah the governor and Ezra the scribe, emerged to inspire and guide the people to rebuild the city, especially its walls and the temple. Nehemiah and Ezra shouldered differing but complementary responsibilities. Nehemiah focused on the city walls and the economic well being of the city. Ezra focused on the temple and the faith of the people.

The long and arduous work of rebuilding the city's physical structures was still underway when this public worship service took place. The service acknowledged that as crucial as the rebuilding effort was, the most important restoration was of the people's hearts and spirits.

The service wasn't held inside the precincts of the reconstructed temple, but on the streets, so that people who could not have gathered inside that holy building could participate. Women and children joined the grown men, and this rare egalitarian gathering was a sign which pointed forward to God's dream for the world made known in Jesus, a world in which everyone is welcome.

All the people came together, and Ezra read to them from their Bible, the part of the Hebrew Scriptures that we know as the Torah or the Pentateuch—the first five books of our Old Testament. As he read, a team of thirteen Levites—think of them as ministers of Christian education or Sunday school teachers—

moved among the people to be sure they understood what they were hearing. It's a reminder of the help we all need as we explore the Bible's meaning for us.

Without Someone to Guide Me, How Could I Understand? (Acts 8:26-31)

We find a similar reminder in the story of Philip's encounter with the Ethiopian eunuch. An angel said to Philip: "At noon, take the road that leads from Jerusalem to Gaza" (Acts 8:26). Philip didn't protest this unexpected assignment. He did what the angel ordered him to do. He traveled the lonely road toward Gaza and met up with a man whose name we never learn. We know him only as the Ethiopian eunuch.

Think of the man from Ethiopia as a seeker after truth who, because of his work as the manager of the queen's treasury, had access to wealth and power, but who yearned for an experience of God's acceptance and love. He was making the long journey back to Ethiopia from a visit to Jerusalem. Ethiopia was far to the south, well past Gaza, and in the region of the Upper Nile. In the popular imagination, "Ethiopia" was beyond the horizon of the familiar, what we might call "Timbuktu" or "the jump-ing-off place."

He was a eunuch, which means he had been castrated, perhaps at an early age. In some parts of the world, though not in Israel, it was common to render a man physically incapable of having sex and then to place him in a position of high authority over the royal family's personal wealth and the king's harem. The indignity done to this man consigned him to a life in which he experienced no fully expressed intimacy, no family, no children, and no real home.

This powerful but lonely man had somehow learned about the God of Israel and he was on a quest to know more. His search took him to Jerusalem. There, the door of the temple was slammed shut against him. He learned from bitter exclusion that the law of Moses prohibited a man like him from entering that holy place. According to Deuteronomy 23:1 and Leviticus 21:17-21, a eunuch had no place in the assembly of the Lord.

Their Bible said it: a man like him could never call the temple his home.

Despite the rejection he underwent, this seeker did not give up his quest to know Israel's God. He purchased some scrolls of the Hebrew Scriptures. On his way back to Ethiopia, he read from them, particularly from the book of Isaiah.

As he read, his chariot passed Philip, who was walking beside the road. The Holy Spirit ordered Philip to run alongside his chariot, and he heard that the Ethiopian was reading from what we know as the 53rd chapter of Isaiah:

> Like a sheep he was led to the slaughter, and like a lamb before its shearer is silent, so he didn't open his mouth. In his humiliation, justice was taken away from him. Who can tell the story of his descendants, because his life was taken from the earth? (Acts 8:32-33; see Isaiah 53:7-8)

A clearer translation of that crucial (for the Ethiopian) last phrase is: "How can he have children, if his life is snatched away?" (Contemporary English Version).

The Ethiopian could identify his own experience with the experience described in Isaiah: the possibility of being a father, of having descendants who would carry on the story of his family, had been taken away from him. Perhaps the Ethiopian had also read further in the writings of Isaiah and had discovered these startling and hopeful words:

> Don't let the eunuch say, "I'm just a dry tree." The Lord says: To the eunuchs who keep my sabbaths, choose what I desire, and remain loyal to my covenant. In my temple and courts, I will give them a monument and a name better than sons and daughters. I will give to them an enduring name that won't be removed. (Isa 56:3-5)

He must have been confused, because he found in the writings of the same prophet words that left him outside the welcome of God and other words that included him in God's house and heart. How was he supposed to make sense out of the Bible when it seemed in tension with itself?

Philip, who was jogging alongside the chariot, asked the Ethiopian, "Do you really understand what you are reading?" (Acts 8:30).

The Ethiopian replied, "Without someone to guide me, how could I?" (v. 31). His question underscores that when interpreting the Bible is a complex challenge, we need the guidance of a wise teacher or a wise community.

The Ethiopian stopped his chariot to pick up Philip. Then he asked him, "Tell me, about whom does the prophet say this? Is he talking about himself or someone else?" (Acts 8:34).

In response, "starting with that passage, Philip proclaimed the good news about Jesus to him" (v. 35).

Philip told him the story of Jesus, which made it clear that God's love embraces people like the Ethiopian eunuch—marginalized, excluded, and lonely. When Jesus was raised from the dead, forgiveness, acceptance, love, and healing flowed freely over the whole world and on all people.

This story offers us a key principle for a Christian understanding of the Bible: the will and way of Jesus, revealed in his words and deeds, are the standard by which we evaluate all other texts and all of our interpretations of texts. If we come away from the Bible with a view of God that is inconsistent with Jesus—if we think God would do or say something Jesus would not say or do—then we haven't yet heard the Bible fully and truthfully. The Bible tells us of a God who is like Jesus, and wise teachers guide us to that gracious and merciful God.

Notes

Notes

3

MISAPPLYING
SCRIPTURE
2 Timothy 2:14-18, 22-26; 2 Peter 3:15-16

Central Question
Do I read the Bible with humility?

Scripture

2 Timothy 2:14-18, 22-26
14 Remind them of these things and warn them in the sight of God not to engage in battles over words that aren't helpful and only destroy those who hear them. 15 Make an effort to present yourself to God as a tried-and-true worker, who doesn't need to be ashamed but is one who interprets the message of truth correctly. 16 Avoid their godless discussions, because they will lead many people into ungodly behavior, 17 and their ideas will spread like an infection. This includes Hymenaeus and Philetus, 18 who have deviated from the truth by claiming that the resurrection has already happened. This has undermined some people's faith.... 22 Run away from adolescent cravings. Instead, pursue righteousness, faith, love, and peace together with those who confess the Lord with a clean heart. 23 Avoid foolish and thoughtless discussions, since you know that they produce conflicts. 24 God's slave shouldn't be argumentative but should be kind toward all people, able to teach, patient, 25 and should correct opponents with gentleness. Perhaps God will change their mind and give them a knowledge of the truth. 26 They may come to their senses and escape from the devil's trap that holds them captive to do his will.

2 Peter 3:15-16

15 Consider the patience of our Lord to be salvation, just as our dear friend and brother Paul wrote to you according to the wisdom given to him, 16 speaking of these things in all his letters. Some of his remarks are hard to understand, and people who are ignorant and whose faith is weak twist them to their own destruction, just as they do the other scriptures.

Reflecting

It was 1969, and I was in the sixth grade when my beloved rural home church hosted an enthusiastic guest preacher. I can still see him running up and down the aisles. I can still see elderly Mr. Wilson sitting serenely until he was jarred to attention by the preacher slapping him on the knee as he ran by.

But the part of the preacher's act that set me to wondering about him came when he launched his Bible from one side of the building in an attempt to land it on the piano on the other side. He missed and his copy of the Good Book hit the floor.

"That," I thought, "doesn't seem like the right way to handle the Bible." It was certainly disrespectful.

Years later, as a grown-up pastor attending a conference hosted by my local Baptist association of churches, I listened to the preacher present a passionate affirmation of his belief in the authority of Scripture. I then listened as he proceeded to offer an interpretation of a Gospel passage that took little account of what the text meant in its historical or its narrative context. He seemed perfectly willing to misuse the text in order to make his point.

"That," I thought, "doesn't seem like the right way to handle the Bible." It was more than disrespectful; it was dangerous because his listeners wanted to hear what the Bible said to them. His careless treatment of the text kept that from happening.

Do we approach the Bible arrogantly, believing that it supports our preconceived notions or that it means whatever we think it means? Or do we approach it humbly with a desire to discover what God has to say to us and with a willingness to do the hard work of understanding it as best we can?

Studying

It isn't certain that Hymenaeus and Philetus derived their belief that the resurrection had already occurred (2 Tim 2:17-18) from the teachings of Paul. It isn't hard to imagine how they might have done so, however (see Gloer, 259–260). Imagine these two listening to Paul's letter to the Colossians being read aloud in church. When the reader gets to Colossians 3:1-3, they hear these words:

> Therefore, if you were raised with Christ, look for the things that are above where Christ is sitting at God's right side. Think about the things above and not things on earth. You died, and your life is hidden with Christ in God.

Hymenaeus is also mentioned in 1 Timothy 1:20 Philetus is mentioned nowhere else in the Bible.

Hymenaeus and Philetus look at each other, their eyes wide. Neither of them hears anything else that is read. After the meeting they discuss what they had heard. Hymenaeus says, "Did you hear that? We have already been raised! The resurrection has already happened! We don't have to wait for it!"

Philetus replies, "Do you see what that means? Maybe it doesn't matter what we do with these old bodies since they're just going to be dust one of these days!" We can imagine how they would excitedly go about sharing their newfound "revelation."

Those of us who have struggled through Paul's letters can sympathize with 2 Peter's admission that some of them can be hard to understand (2 Pet 3:15-16). So we can sympathize with Hymenaeus and Philetus's confusion. Though we have no first-hand knowledge of the state of these men's hearts or of their motives in sharing their belief that the resurrection had already occurred, we do have Paul's judgment that they had "deviated from the truth" to the detriment of the faith of many (2 Tim 2:16-18). Paul warned Timothy, and by extension us, to stay away from such activity because of its damaging results.

In the imaginary scenario above, Hymenaeus and Philetus committed an all-too-common error in biblical interpretation: they pulled the passage that attracted their attention out of its context. How much more correct would their understanding have been had they just listened to Paul's next sentence: "When Christ, who is your life, is revealed, then you also will be revealed with him in glory" (Col 3:4). Their teaching that those in Christ were already living the resurrected life wouldn't have been a problem had it been balanced with teaching about the resurrection yet to come.

The error of these men was one of interpretation. Their failure to take the overall teaching of Paul into account led them to overemphasize the present aspect of his teaching about resurrection and neglect the future aspect.

Perhaps they appealed to the "plain sense" of what they heard Paul say, presumably taking the text literally by getting back to its basic, commonsense meaning without any need for interpretation. The problem is that there is no such thing as reading without interpretation; reading is itself an act of interpretation. Both of this week's texts acknowledge as much, 2 Peter in its observation that Paul's words could be difficult to understand and Paul in his encouragement to Timothy to be a faithful interpreter of God's truth (2 Tim 2:15).

Paul encourages Timothy toward ethical biblical interpretation. He prods Timothy to let his motives and practices in interpreting the Bible come out of his ever-maturing Christian identity. In the same way, our Christian identity should determine how we study the Bible and what we make of what we learn in such study. Based on Paul's instructions in 2 Timothy 2, what might we learn about such study?

First, ethical biblical interpretation emphasizes the saving act of God in Jesus Christ (v. 14). Paul told Timothy to remind the people of the basics of the gospel that he had summarized earlier in the chapter: "Remember Jesus Christ, who was raised from the dead and descended from David. This is my good news" (2 Tim 2:8). We should concentrate on the majors and not get hung up on disputes over the minors.

Second, ethical biblical interpretation involves disciplined effort (v. 16). Paul encouraged Timothy to be a true artisan in his studies so he could be proud of his efforts to arrive at the truth (Oden, 66). There is no substitute for doing the hard and serious work of Bible study. We should use the best tools we have available. Though most of us don't have advanced degrees in biblical studies or theology, we can read the works of those who do. We should seek the best help we can find. The material for deep Bible study is there if only we are willing to use it.

Third, ethical biblical interpretation seeks to do good and not harm. Paul encouraged Timothy to "avoid their godless discussions, because they will lead many people into ungodly behavior" (v. 16). Such discussions create harmful teachings that could spread like a virus through the church and harm people's faith (vv. 17-18). The point of our Bible study should be to build up and not to tear down.

Fourth, ethical biblical interpretation is other-focused, not self-centered. The Christian interpreter of Scripture cares more about building and maintaining loving relationships with others than about fulfilling an immature need to feel superior to others. Thus, Paul encouraged Timothy to "run away from adolescent cravings" and instead to run toward "righteousness, faith, love, and peace together with those who confess the Lord with a clean heart" (v. 22). Ethical Bible study leads to the development of Christian community. It is motivated by a desire to be loving rather than by a need to be right (vv. 24-25).

Finally, ethical biblical interpretation leaves the outcomes in God's hands. It is our job to share lovingly and graciously; it is God's job to convict and to convince (vv. 25-26). There is no place for manipulation or for coercion as we share with others the message of the Bible.

Understanding

Hymenaeus and Philetus's problem wasn't that they misunderstood the teaching of Paul. As 2 Peter says, Paul's words can be hard for anyone to understand. Instead, their problem was that their interpretation of Paul's teachings did not take God fully into account and, as a result, they were damaging people's faith, with their harmful teaching spreading like a virulent disease.

In other words, they were more interested in their own understandings and ideas than they were in God's truth, and they were more interested in promoting their understanding and ideas than they were with the well-being of God's church. They were, in short, more interested in their own things than in the things of God. They were too clever for their own good—and for the church's good. Their approach was driven by arrogance rather than by humility.

Paul encouraged Timothy to approach the Scriptures differently. He encouraged Timothy to do the hard work of Bible study so his interpretations would be correct. In essence, he should approach Scripture with the assumption that he doesn't know all the truth, but that he can find it through diligent study. The goal was for Timothy to present himself to God without being ashamed.

No matter how much we grow in our understanding of Scripture and of the God who stands behind Scripture, we will always have a long way to go. That realization should motivate us to a humble approach to the Bible that cares more about God, truth, and the church than about our particular insights.

What About Me?

• *Do I study the Bible faithfully and regularly?* If we really believe the Bible contains and points to God's truth, it only makes sense to come to it in an ongoing and disciplined way. Conversely, not to come to it would indicate that we don't really think we need it.

• *Do I study the Bible because I want to know as much of God's truth as possible?* If we really believe that Scripture tells us about God's saving acts, we'll want to know as much as we can about what God has done so we can better detect what God is still doing. We especially want to know as much as possible about what God did in the life, death, and resurrection of Jesus so we can live—and help others to live—in ways that reflect what it means to follow Jesus here and now.

• *Do I study the Bible assuming it may not be easy to understand yet trusting that God will guide me?* Some parts of the Bible are simply hard to understand. Furthermore, some parts that seem easy to understand—that seem obvious at face value or seem clear because we've always heard them interpreted a certain way—are actually not so easy. It's best to come to Scripture with open minds, hearts, and lives, asking God for help in understanding.

• *Do I study the Bible in order to do good and not harm others?* If we have serious doubts about something we think we find in Scripture, it is best to keep it to ourselves until we can see more clearly. But even a truth of which we are firmly convinced can be harmful if we share or use it the wrong way. Grace and love should be the guiding lights in our biblical interpretation.

Resources

W. Hulitt Gloer, *1 & 2 Timothy-Titus*, Smyth & Helwys Bible Commentary (Macon GA: Smyth & Helwys, 2010).

Thomas C. Oden, *First and Second Timothy and Titus*, Interpretation: A Bible Commentary for Teaching and Preaching (Louisville KY: John Knox, 1989).

N. T. Wright, *The Last Word: Beyond the Bible Wars to a New Understanding of the Authority of Scripture* (San Francisco: Harper, 2005).

MISAPPLYING
SCRIPTURE
2 Timothy 2:14-18, 22-26; 2 Peter 3:15-16

Ways to Read—and Ways Not to Read—the Bible

In this unit of lessons, we're thinking about the gift of the Scriptures, about the work of scholars and translators who make them available and accessible to us, and about how God speaks to us through their unmistakable humanity. Today, we consider the attitudes of mind and heart that make us receptive to God's word.

There are many ways to read the Bible. We can read it as a literary classic, which it clearly is. It has given us many of the master plots and much of the enduring imagery of great Western literature.

We can read the Bible as a collection of stories and a compendium of wisdom about the human condition. Its insights are probing and illuminating.

We can even read the Bible as an aid to our understanding of history, particularly the history of Israel and of the early church, although we have to keep in mind that the writers of Scripture did not intend to write the kind of objective history we expect from modern historians. They didn't write straightforwardly about what happened, but rather about the meaning of what happened. The Scriptures are an interpretation of history even more than they are a *description* of history.

There are also many ways *not* to read the Bible. The Bible isn't *a scientific textbook*. To read it as a source of knowledge about physics and biology is to misread it and to set up unnecessary conflicts between science and faith. The Bible tells us about the gift of creation and about the loving God whose handiwork it is, not about the detailed processes God used to fashion our beautiful world.

The Bible isn't *a collection of rules*, though there are certainly many laws and rules in its pages. It's crucial, though, to remember that those laws and rules are always part of a broader and unfolding story of God's desire to teach human beings to live with one another in harmony and justice and to treat each other with dignity and respect. Without the broader story—and the awareness that the story isn't yet finished—we can become narrow-minded, small-hearted legalists who use the laws and rules to condemn and control others. We run the risk of making it seem that God is a harsh law-and-order judge whose main purpose is to convict and punish us for our mistakes and sins. We can forget that even God's judgment is an expression of God's love. It is part of God's hope that we will stop living in ways that harm us, others, and the creation.

Furthermore, the Bible isn't *a self-help book* filled with principles and inspiration to help us change ourselves by our own efforts and the strength of our own willpower. The well-known adage "God helps those who help themselves" is commonly thought to be a scriptural proverb, but it isn't. It appears in various versions: in the teachings of ancient Greek philosophers, in Aesop's fables, and in *Poor Richard's Almanac*. It is a religious sentiment, but the religion it encapsulates isn't Christianity. The Bible describes a God who comes to us in Jesus and redeems us when we are down and out, when we have hit bottom and can't climb or crawl our way up, and when we are absolutely helpless.

A Relational Approach to Scripture

I believe that the Holy Spirit invites us to read the Bible as the faithful telling and retelling of a great love story: the story of God's gracious love for the whole world. We can trust the Scriptures to guide us into a life that experiences and expresses that divine love. To say something obvious but sometimes overlooked, the Bible is God's *story*, but it is not God. Our purpose in reading the Bible is to know and be known by, to love and be loved by, the God whose story the Bible tells. Strictly speaking, our relationship is with God, not with the Bible. New Testament scholar Scot McKnight describes a "relational approach to the Bible" in these terms:

> The relational approach *distinguishes God from the Bible*. God existed before the Bible existed; God exists independently of the Bible now. God is a person; the Bible is paper. God gave us this papered Bible to lead us to love his person. But the persona and the paper are not the same.... We want to emphasize that we don't ask what the Bible says, we ask what God says to us in the Bible. The difference is a difference between papers and person.... God gave us the Bible not so we can know it but so we can know and love God through it. (Scot McKnight, *The Blue Parakeet* [Grand Rapids MI: Zondervan, 2008] 87, 91)

We call the Bible the *written* word of God because it reliably and powerfully puts us in touch with the *living* Word of God, Jesus.

When we read the Scriptures with an open mind and an open heart—especially when we read them in a community of fellow seekers and with the help of sound scholarship—they will lead us to Jesus and the kind of life he dreams for us to have. For Christians, the Scriptures speak with his voice. As Jesus said to a group of religious leaders in Jerusalem: "Examine the scriptures, since you think that in them you have eternal life. They also testify about me" (John 5:39).

Avoid Battles Over Words (2 Tim 2:14-18, 22-26)

When the Apostle Paul wrote to Timothy, his younger protégé and colleague in ministry, he offered him guidance about how to approach the responsibility of teaching. Paul was particularly concerned that Timothy set an example of reading and interpreting the Bible with humility and teaching it with love. Some members of the church in Ephesus (where Timothy ministered in Paul's absence) had turned their shared exploration of the Scriptures into an arena of contentious debate. They had introduced conflict into what should have been a holy conversation conducted in mutual respect and committed to discerning God's voice. Paul urged Timothy to "warn them in the sight of God not to engage in battles over words that aren't helpful and only destroy those who hear them" (2 Tim 2:14).

Apparently, there were teachers, or would-be teachers, in the church who insisted that others agree entirely with their understanding of Scripture. They wanted everyone to conform to their precise vocabulary and phrasing of the truth as they understood it. They were insistent that people agree with them, their views, and their terminology. The study of Scripture had become a destructive argument.

Paul wanted Timothy to "avoid their godless discussions, because they will lead many people into ungodly behavior, and their ideas will spread like an infection" (2:16-17). It was so important that Timothy steer clear of this kind of pointless and poisonous conflict that Paul repeated the advice just a few verses later: "Avoid foolish and thoughtless discussions, since you know that they produce conflicts" (v. 23).

Paul called the discussions of the controversial teachers "godless" because the goal of those discussions wasn't actually to hear from God. Instead, their purpose was to hear the echo of their own voices in the forced compliance into which they strong-armed those they taught.

Paul pointed out to Timothy that godless discussions lead to ungodly behavior. It's sobering to realize that there is a connection between the ways we talk, especially about matters of the Spirit, and the ways we live. To speak godlessly leads to godless actions, but to speak humbly after listening to one another and to God leads to peaceful and respectful behavior. Our words and deeds are vitally and inevitably connected.

Paul encouraged Timothy to present himself to God "as a tried-and-true worker, who doesn't need to be ashamed but is one who interprets the message of truth correctly" (v. 15). "Tried-and-true" workers have spent time learning and practicing their craft, often under the tutelage of a master craftsperson who has enriched the workers' abilities with his or her own knowledge and experience. An "unashamed" worker consistently produces quality goods and services. He or she has an unwavering commitment to excellence. Timothy had learned about the craft of teaching from Paul himself, and Paul urged him to give his best to the task of protecting the people under his care from the "infection" (v. 17) of bad teaching and of guiding them to health-giving ways of understanding Scripture.

An unashamed worker is one who, according to the Common English Bible, "interprets the message of truth correctly" (v. 15). Similarly, the New Revised Standard Version offers this translation: "rightly explaining the word of truth." Both translations accurately convey the meaning of Paul's words, but they obscure a helpful metaphor he used. We could render Paul's words as "cutting a clear and straight path to the word of truth." As James D. G. Dunn puts it, Paul's image is

> of cutting a path straight across forested or rough country, so that travelers can go directly to their destination. So the thought presumably is either of cutting a straight path for the gospel or of leading the unwary through thickets or uneven ground in the tradition that otherwise might cause them to lose their direction. ("First and Second Letters to Timothy," *The New Interpreter's Bible*, vol. 11 [Nashville TN: Abingdon, 2000] 844)

Faithful teachers of God's word "shouldn't be argumentative but should be kind toward all people, able to teach, patient, and should correct opponents with gentleness. Perhaps God will change their mind and give them a knowledge of the truth. They may come to their senses and escape from the devil's trap that holds them captive to do his will" (vv. 24-26). Here, Paul makes it clear that the most effective teaching has to do with Christlike character even more than skill. As the preceding verses demonstrate, however, skill matters greatly. Christian teachers are called to love those whom they teach—love evidenced by kindness, patience, and gentleness.

It's especially noteworthy that Paul told Timothy to be loving toward those who differed from him: "correct opponents with gentleness" (v. 25). It wasn't up to Timothy to change their minds, only to speak the truth clearly and lovingly. Any change that might occur was God's work, not Timothy's: "Perhaps God will change their mind" (v. 25). In our own time, when the climate of conversation among Christians is often heated and when disagreements rapidly lead to disruptions and even divisions of faith communities, it would help us to recall that our responsibility is simply to bear loving witness to the truth as we understand it. We aren't responsible for changing people's views or for persuading them to agree with us.

Some Things in Scripture Are Hard to Understand (2 Pet 3:15-18)

The writer of 2 Peter had seen that people can twist the Scriptures in a way that is destructive to them. He thought people were especially prone to that kind of misuse when they encountered passages that were hard to understand (2 Pet 3:16). He admitted that even he found some obscure and difficult texts in the writings of Paul! I find that admission to be one of the most delightfully human statements in the New Testament.

It also suggests an important principle for our engagement with Scripture: we should spend most of our time and energy applying the clear and challenging words of Scripture to how we live, not on fruitless speculation about the meaning of elusive texts.

As Mark Twain famously said, "It ain't those parts of the Bible that I can't understand that bother me, it is the parts that I do understand."

The purpose of Bible study, like the purpose of other disciplines and practices of Christian living, is to enable us to "grow in the grace and knowledge of our Lord and savior Jesus Christ. To him belongs glory now and forever. Amen" (2 Pet 3:18).

Notes

Notes

4

READING
WITH UNDERSTANDING
Matthew 22:34-40; Acts 17:10-12

Central Question
Do I take the Bible seriously?

Scripture

Matthew 22:34-40
34 When the Pharisees heard that Jesus had left the Sadducees speechless, they met together. 35 One of them, a legal expert, tested him. 36 "Teacher, what is the greatest commandment in the Law?" 37 He replied, "You must love the Lord your God with all your heart, with all your being, and with all your mind. 38 This is the first and greatest commandment. 39 And the second is like it: You must love your neighbor as you love yourself. 40 All the Law and the Prophets depend on these two commands."

Acts 17:10-12
10 As soon as it was dark, the brothers and sisters sent Paul and Silas on to Beroea. When they arrived, they went to the Jewish synagogue. 11 The Beroean Jews were more honorable than those in Thessalonica. This was evident in the great eagerness with which they accepted the word and examined the scriptures each day to see whether Paul and Silas' teaching was true. 12 Many came to believe, including a number of reputable Greek women and many Greek men.

Reflecting

Dr. J. J. Owens, who died in 2002, was a longtime professor of Old Testament at the Southern Baptist Theological Seminary. I took several classes with him in the 1its divine message comes to us through human writers, editors, compilers, and translators. It means taking seriously both what humans and God have to say about it. And it means taking seriously that we best interpret it only when we invest our lives in an ongoing conversation with it, with the Spirit of the Lord, with the world around us, and with the Christian community.

Studying

The Bible deserves our careful study. The Beroean Jews in Acts 17 listened to Paul preach about Jesus. Then they set about studying their Scriptures. Let us not look past the seemingly simple fact that they read their Bibles. The Bible has no meaning for us until we read it. It is not a monument to be admired or an idol to be venerated. Rather, it is one of God's primary ways of drawing us into the story of salvation, into a maturing relationship with Christ, and into the very life of God.

We should consider the scope of the Bible that we read. Hopefully, the other lessons in this unit have given us a greater appreciation for the wonderful gift that God has given us through the work of God's Spirit in partnership with human speakers and writers. The entire Bible is a gift, so we should read the entire Bible that we have.

Different groups have different Bibles, though. The Bible of the legal expert who asked Jesus about the greatest commandment (Matt 22:34-40) was the Hebrew Old Testament. His Bible would have included all or most of what we find in our Old Testaments. We can be reasonably sure that since Beroea was in Greece, the Bible that the Beroean Jews studied was the Greek Old Testament, most likely some version of the Septuagint.

So the Pharisees studied a Bible that was more or less like ours, just in a different language. The Beroeans studied a Bible that likely included some additional books that came to be included in the Greek Bible but were not in the Hebrew Bible. We designate these books as "Apocrypha."

The Christian Bible contains the books of the Old and New Testaments. For Protestants, the Old Testament contains the same materials found in the Jewish Bible. Roman Catholics and Orthodox Christians, however, include the Apocrypha in their Old Testament—although not all groups recognize the same books.

The books of our Old Testament were evidently considered canonical in Judaism by the time the Romans destroyed Jerusalem in AD 70. The earliest list we have of the books that now make up our New Testament appears in a letter written by Bishop Athanasius of Alexandria in AD 367. Although there were discussions among church leaders about what books were and were not authoritative, for the most part communities of faith made these decisions practically by accepting and using some books and not others.

The point of this very brief survey of the biblical canon is that by the grace of God, through the guidance of the Holy Spirit, and through the contributions of many faithful people who preserved and used the books, we have the entire Bible from Genesis to Revelation available to us. We need to study the entire book.

We should use the best tools available to us in our study of the Bible. We are fortunate to live in a time when there are many print and digital resources to help us in our study. Not all resources are of equal value, though, and we need to be discerning about what we use and whom we trust. Like the Beroeans, we must search out whether the things others teach us are true. To do so, perhaps we can apply the same standard Jesus gave the legal expert in his quest of the greatest commandment: does it point us toward love? We might also take a cue from our lesson two weeks ago

> While the "canon" of scripture means the list of books accepted as holy scripture, the other sense of "canon"—rule or standard—has rubbed off on this one, so that the "canon" of scripture is understood to be the list of books which are acknowledged to be, in a unique sense, the rule of belief and practice. (Bruce, 18)

about Philip's encounter with the Ethiopian official and ask, "Does it point us to Christ?" Those criteria should guide not only our evaluation of the available study aids but also our study of the biblical text.

The legal expert who asked Jesus to identify the greatest commandment did so as part of a conspiracy to entrap Jesus. His question nonetheless reflected a genuine interest of the biblical scholars of his day, namely, what was to be the controlling truth in their study and application of the law? They sought the heart of the Torah, in the light of which they could best understand the teachings of their Scripture and live them out.

In his answer, Jesus pointed the legal expert and his fellows toward a life of love. He said loving the Lord with everything you are and loving your neighbor as yourself together formed the heart of a life lived under God. Since the interpretation and application of the entire Bible ("the Law and the Prophets" constituted the entire Bible for Jesus' audience) depended on such love, the proper way to read the Bible is with an eye toward how to understand and obey the Bible so that love is the guiding principle of life.

The best way to put love at the center of our biblical interpretation is to have Christ as the center of our lives, because in Christ we best see and experience the love of God and of others. Jesus loved his heavenly Father and his earthly brothers and sisters so much that he willingly laid down his life in service to them. As we learn to keep Christ and his love at the center of our Bible reading, perhaps we will grow toward being the self-emptying and other-serving people God calls us to be through Scripture, Jesus, and the Spirit. "To be a Christian is to be called to a life of love," Stanley Hauerwas writes, "but that calling is a lifelong task that requires our willingness to be surprised by what love turns out to be" (194).

> Love is total commitment that thinks more of the divine Other and of the human other than it does of the self.

Scripture presents us with an opportunity to grow in our knowledge of God in Christ so that we can grow in leading a life

of love. To take the Bible seriously grows out of our commitment to take our relationship with God and with each other seriously.

We can't do such reading on our own, however. We need the help of other people and of the Spirit of God. To take the Bible seriously, then, is to read it both carefully and prayerfully.

Understanding

Most people would say that what matters most is having a life that has meaning and purpose. Christians believe that we have found the key to such a life in our relationship with God through Jesus Christ our Lord. If that relationship is indeed the key to life, then it seems logical that we would make full use of whatever means God has given us to deepen and to develop that life.

Along with worship, prayer, and participation in the Christian community, the Bible is one of the most important means that God has given us to help us to grow in our relationship with God. So we really need to read our Bible. Considering that our relationship with God is what gives meaning to our lives, surely we want to read it well and in such a way that it will best help us grow in our relationship with God.

How do we best read the Bible? We best read it with Jesus Christ at the center of our reading. The Beroeans diligently studied their Bibles to see if what Paul said about Jesus was true. Christians have indeed found that what Paul and the other biblical writers say about Jesus is true. Today we read our Bible to find out all that we can about Jesus Christ as the center of God's saving acts and as the center of our lives. Moreover, since Jesus is the culmination of God's saving acts, we read our Bible through

the lens of the actions, teachings, death, and resurrection of Jesus.

We best read the Bible with love as the goal of our reading. Love of God and love for people is, after all, what Jesus said is the goal of studying the Bible and living out its teachings. Love is also the goal of our lives as Christians.

What About Me?

• *Does the effort I put into studying my Bible indicate that I take it seriously?* Do we venerate the Bible or do we study it? Do we believe things about it or do we believe what it tells us about God and about our relationships with God and others?

• *Does my view of the biblical canon indicate that I take the Bible seriously?* While you may have never given much thought to the canon, the truth is that we all have a "canon within the canon." That is, we all have books or passages to which we pay more attention than we do others. How can you move toward taking the entire Bible more seriously?

• *Does what I put at the heart of my Bible study indicate that I take it seriously?* Do I put self at the center by viewing the Bible as a book on how to improve my life? Do I put tradition at the center, viewing the Bible as a collection of proof texts? Or do I put Jesus at the center? Do I view the Bible as the story of God's great saving activity that culminates in Jesus? Do I read the Bible through the lens of Jesus or through some lesser lens?

• *Does the goal of my Bible study indicate that I take it seriously?* After all, the Bible says that Jesus is the Messiah, the Son of the living God who came to take away the sins of the world. And according to the Bible, Jesus the Messiah said that the goal of life should be to love God with all we are and to love our neighbor as ourselves. Do I read the Bible with the goal of following Jesus more and more closely and loving God and people more and more deeply?

Resources

F. F. Bruce, *The Canon of Scripture* (Downers Grove IL: InterVarsity, 1988).

Richard Foster with Kathryn A. Helmers, *Life with God: Reading the Bible for Spiritual Transformation* (New York: HarperOne, 2008).

Stanley Hauerwas, *Matthew*, Brazos Theological Commentary on the Bible (Grand Rapids MI: Brazos, 2006).

READING
WITH UNDERSTANDING
Matthew 22:34-40; Acts 17:10-12

"The Bible Is Holiness in Words"

Today we complete our unit on the many gifts we receive as we faithfully read and study the Scriptures. We've acknowledged the complex tasks of establishing and translating biblical texts, tasks for which most of us need the help of skilled scholars. We've seen the importance of approaching the Scriptures with an awareness that they are in one sense inevitably human but in another inspiringly divine. We've reflected on the crucial attitudes of openness, humility, and peacefulness with which we study the Bible, especially as we study it in conversation with others.

These lessons have underscored for me the profound truth of a statement by Abraham Joshua Heschel, a remarkable twentieth-century rabbi:

> The Bible is holiness in words.... It is as if God took these Hebrew words and breathed into them of His power, and the words became a live wire charged with His Spirit. To this very day, they are hyphens between heaven and earth. (*God in Search of Man: A Philosophy of Judaism* [New York: Macmillan, 1976] 244)

We would, of course, include the Greek words of the New Testament in our celebration of the ways in which the Bible is "holiness in words" and "hyphens between heaven and earth."

Sometimes, followers of Jesus wonder how to make a case for the Bible. They want to know what arguments they can make and what evidence they can present in order to convince people that it is, despite all its human characteristics, God's written word. My view is that we don't need such arguments and that the kind of evidence we could present wouldn't finally be persuasive. I think the Bible makes its own case, and we simply need to ask people to read it with an open mind and, perhaps, in a group. Since it is, as Heschel says, "charged with God's Spirit," and since it makes more sense out of the human condition than any other collection of writings, it will speak convincingly for itself. More precisely, God will speak searchingly and lovingly *through* the Bible. When we hear God speak to us by means of the Scriptures, that experience persuades us of their authenticity and authority more certainly than any argument could.

Today's lesson calls us to reaffirm our commitment to diligent and transformational study of the Bible and to renew our willingness to hear in its words an ongoing invitation to a relationship of trust and love with God. Another twentieth-century student of the Bible, the Congregationalist preacher Browne Barr, said that the Scriptures sound

> a melody that will not be silenced despite many poor notes, bad notes, wrong notes, hesitations and repeats sounded by the human musicians. [Its center] is Jesus, the Christ, the cruci- fied and risen Lord, who has in his hands the print of those nails which go through to the hands and heart of God. ("Hang Tough," *The Christian Century*, 11 April 1979).

For Christians, the central melody of the Bible is the love of God made known to us in the life, teachings, death, and resurrection of Jesus. We read and study it in order to hear that music.

Examining the Scriptures Each Day (Acts 17:10-12)

Acts 17 contains Paul's well-known speech to a crowd of philosophers in Athens (17:16-26), a speech he gave in a secular place, the Areopagus, where the city's philosophical and political leaders often gathered for debate. He began his speech not, as he often did, with a text from the Hebrew Bible, but with a reference to "objects of worship" (v. 23) he had seen in their marketplace and to a line from an Athenian poet (v. 28). He presented his reasons for trusting in God as the Creator (vv. 24-28) and as the One who raised Jesus from the dead (v. 31). Some who listened to Paul ridiculed him. Others promised to hear him again (v. 32), and a few became believers (v. 34).

Before arriving in Athens, Paul and his traveling companion, Silas, made their way across Macedonia, stopping first in Thessalonica (vv. 1-9) and then Beroea (vv. 10-12). In both cities, Paul went to the synagogue and spoke about Jesus as the Messiah on the basis of texts from the Hebrew Scriptures. In Thessalonica, he demonstrated from Scripture that "the Christ had to suffer and rise from the dead" (Acts 17:3). From there, he proclaimed Jesus to them (v. 3). Although some of the people who heard Paul speak were convinced (v. 4), the overwhelming response in the synagogue was negative and became violent. There was a riot, instigated by the Jewish leaders among "thugs" in the marketplace. Paul and Silas were charged with disturbing the peace (vv. 5-6). As quickly as they could, Paul and Silas left Thessalonica and went to Beroea, about fifty miles southwest of Thessalonica, in the foothills of the Olympian mountains.

It's likely that Luke (the author of Acts) wrote about the violent reaction of the Thessalonians to Paul and Silas to heighten the contrast between the welcome they and their message received in Beroea and the mixed but nonviolent response they received in Athens. Paul and Silas went to the Beroean synagogue and found the people who gathered to hear them to be "more honorable than those in Thessalonica" (17:11). "Honorable" here means something like "fair-minded" or "willing to consider new ideas." For reasons unknown to us, they were less fearful of the possibility that what they heard would require a change in their thinking. The evidence of their honorable attitude was "the great eagerness with which they accepted the word and examined the scriptures each day to see whether Paul and Silas' teaching was true" (17:11).

The Beroean example is one for us to follow: listen to what scholars, teachers, ministers, colleagues, and friends think about the Scriptures. Then, on the basis of personal study, come to our own conclusions about the message God has for us. I don't hear this phrase much any more, but as a boy I sometimes heard preachers challenge the congregation to "be like the Beroeans." In other words, "Check out for yourself the things I am saying to you. Don't believe it because I say it. Believe it only if the Bible says it to *you*." Even though I doubt any of them thought their hearers would study the Scriptures and come to a different conclusion than theirs, there was wisdom and even humility in this call for us to "be like the Beroeans." For our faith to be ours, we need to engage the Scriptures with both the freedom and responsibility to come to our own conclusions about what God says to us through them.

Love for God and Neighbor (Matt 22:34-40)

Jesus' engagement with the Bible led him to the conclusion that its central message was love. For Jesus, "the Bible" was especially the Torah, the first five books of our Old Testament, and also, but secondarily, the books of the prophets and the other writings such as Job, Psalms, Proverbs, and Ecclesiastes. The tradition of Bible study in which Jesus was nurtured valued discussion and debate—the give and take of ideas, opinions, and questions— as ways of discerning the meaning of Scripture texts.

Matthew's Gospel recounts a conversation between Jesus and a Pharisee who was also a legal expert, one whose special focus of study was interpreting the law of Moses. Matthew frames the conversation as a test, but that doesn't mean it had a testy tone or that it was a trial of Jesus. It could simply have been a test in the sense of a classroom examination—an attempt to ascertain the range and depth of Jesus' knowledge. Certainly the conversation was in the rich Jewish tradition of arriving at an understanding of the meaning of Moses' writings by means of exchanging viewpoints and even arguing with one another's conclusions.

By the time of Jesus, Jewish scholars and teachers were well on their way to a codification of the teachings of the Torah into 613 commandments, 248 of them stated positively ("You shall") and 365 stated negatively ("You shall not"). While they were codifying the Torah, the scholars and teachers were also debating with each other about which of these commandments were "heavy" (necessary and always binding) and which were "light" (important but could be implemented flexibly, depending on the circumstances). In addition, some of them were searching for a clear summary of the Torah's essential wisdom that could guide the interpretation and application of its varied commands in everyday life.

When the legal expert asked Jesus, "Teacher, what is the greatest commandment in the Law?" (Matt 22:36), it's likely that he wanted to know what the "heaviest" commandment was—the commandment Jesus deemed to be most essential. Jesus began his response by drawing *from the Shema*: "*You must love the Lord your God with all your heart, with all your being,* and with all your mind" (v. 37, citing Deut 6:5). The "first and greatest commandment" (v. 38), Jesus said, is to love God wholly and unreservedly, with every part of your personhood.

Jesus went on to say, "And the second is like it: *You must love your neighbor as you love yourself*" (v. 39, citing Lev 19:18). By saying that this second commandment is like the first, Jesus joined them into an inseparable unity. The greatest commandment is really two. One calls us to the delightful duty of loving God and the other commissions us to the redemptive responsibility of loving others as we love ourselves. Love is what God wants for, and expects from, everyone.

God loves us, and when we catch a glimpse of the wonder of God's love for us, we want to love God in return. God forgives us, liberates us, heals us, empowers us, gladdens us, sustains us, and never forsakes us. God is determined to fill us with hope and joy. God's great love for us invites our great love in return.

The love we experience from God enables us to love ourselves genuinely and gratefully, and that love flows through us to others. Learning to love others pushes outside the tight confines of our limited selves. Love will not let us rest easy in our prejudices, provincialisms, and parochialisms. Love moves out into a world that is vaster and more complicated than the secluded little villages of our settled but unexamined assumptions. Love won't allow us to sort people by stereotypes so we can dismiss them. It requires us instead to see people as individuals with stories, hopes, hurts, disappointments, dreams, adversities, and aspirations and to care for them with mercy and grace.

For Jesus, the heart of Scripture—its essential message and meaning—was love: love for God and love for neighbor. Love is the source and center of the Scriptures because they bear witness to the God who is love (1 John 4:8).

In the shadows of Hitler's Third Reich, Dietrich Bonhoeffer urged the ministers he mentored to listen to the Scriptures as God's message of love for them. He didn't want them to make the error of coming to the Bible simply for the purpose of preparing their next lesson or sermon. He wanted them to let the words of Scripture mediate God's love for them. Bonhoeffer's wisdom is for all of us:

The Word of Scripture should never stop sounding in your ears and working in you all day long, just like the words of someone you love. And just as you do not analyze the words of someone you love, but accept them as they are said to you, accept the Word of Scripture and ponder it in your heart as Mary did. That is all. That is meditation.... Do not ask, "How shall I pass this on?" but, "What does it say to me?" Then ponder this Word long in your heart until it has gone right into you and taken possession of you. (*Life Together* [Minneapolis MN: Fortress, 1996] 62)

Notes

Notes

www.ingramcontent.com/pod-product-compliance
Lightning Source LLC
Chambersburg PA
CBHW060708030426
42337CB00017B/2802